WONDERS
OF THE **WORLD**

Northern Lights

Other books in the Wonders of the World series include:

WONDERS
OF THE WORLD

Northern Lights

Deborah Underwood

KIDHAVEN
PRESS™

THOMSON
™
GALE

San Diego • Detroit • New York • San Francisco • Cleveland
New Haven, Conn. • Waterville, Maine • London • Munich

LIBRARY OF CONGRESS CATALOGING-IN-PUBLICATION DATA

Underwood, Deborah
    Northern Lights / by Deborah Underwood
        p. cm. -- (Wonders of the world)
Includes bibliographical references.
Summary: Discusses the northern lights including how they form, where they appear, myths and legends, and the problems they can cause on Earth.
ISBN 0-7377-2085-9
 1. Auroras--Juvenile literature. [1. Auroras.] I. Title. II. Wonders of the World (KidHaven Press)
QC971.4.U53 2004
538'.768—dc22

                                  2003023206

CONTENTS

What Are the Northern Lights?

A shimmering curtain of light hangs in the night sky. Green and glowing, it billows as if blown by a silent breeze. A golden river snakes up through the heavens, and bright pink flames seem to lick at the horizon. As midnight approaches, the green curtain folds over on itself again and again. It swirls and tumbles across the sky in a blaze of colors before finally breaking up and fading into the night.

The northern lights are surely one of nature's most spectacular shows. They have awed, frightened, and amazed people for thousands of years. People travel long distances and brave freezing temperatures in hopes of getting a glimpse of them. Their eerie beauty captivates even those who have seen them hundreds of times. During particularly bright displays, cars pull over to the side of the road and restaurants empty as people go outside to watch the lights dance.

Shifting Shapes and Colors

Pulsing clouds of light, rays darting down from the heavens like lightning, sheets fluttering and twisting, explosions of swirling lines—the northern lights can appear in any of these forms. Greens and reds are the most common colors, but sometimes purple curls, yellow streaks, or blue flames fill the skies. The constantly shifting patterns and shades make the northern lights fascinating to watch. No two displays are ever exactly alike.

At times, the northern lights are simply a small patch of light, like a strange cloud glowing in the night

The northern lights have frightened and amazed people for thousands of years.

sky. The patch might shine steadily, or it might gently pulse on and off. Sometimes the whole sky seems to be covered with a veil of white light.

But the northern lights often take a more predictable form. The show begins with a glow in the north. Then an arc of light curves across the sky like a greenish white rainbow. As the arc begins to move, it becomes a band with folds or bumps along its bottom edge. Sometimes several arcs or bands reach from horizon to horizon.

Greens and reds are the most common colors of northern lights, and the display of color often begins as a glow in the north.

The bands may stretch into one or more curtains. Curtains have vertical rays extending from their tops to their bottoms, like the folds in a fabric curtain hanging from a window. The curtains can stretch thousands of miles across the sky. They can be several hundred miles tall, but are usually less than a mile thick. If the curtains are viewed from directly underneath, the lights seem to jump out in all directions like a sunburst.

The northern lights are often most active in the few hours before and after midnight. Sometimes after the lights fade, another arc forms and the show begins again. If the lights are especially bright one night, they are likely to be bright the following night, too.

Where the Northern Lights Are Seen

The northern lights are sometimes called the aurora borealis, which means "dawn of the north." As their name suggests, much of the time they appear only in the far north. People in parts of Alaska, northern Canada, Greenland, Iceland, Norway, Finland, and Siberia see the lights quite often.

The northern lights most often appear in the **auroral zone**, an imaginary oval-shaped ring that sits on top of the globe. People living near the auroral zone can view the northern lights on just about any dark, clear night. The farther a place is from the auroral zone, the smaller the chance of seeing the northern lights.

The area where the northern lights occur at any given time is called the **auroral oval**. The oval is usually about twenty-five hundred miles across. Unlike the auroral zone, the auroral oval is not imaginary. With special equipment, it can be seen from space.

Although the lights most often appear in the far north, when the conditions are right the northern lights can be seen farther south. The northern lights are powered by particles from the sun. When the sun shoots off extra particles, the auroral oval stretches down like a rubber band and covers more of the world. On very rare occasions, even people as far south as Mexico can see the northern lights.

Whenever the northern lights are shining, a similar display, the southern lights, or aurora australis, is taking place near the south pole. Most of the time, the only land that the southern auroral oval touches is Antarctica. Since hardly anyone lives on that freezing continent, very few people ever see the southern lights.

By photographing the northern and southern lights at the same time, scientists have learned that their colors and patterns are often exact mirror images of each other. Together the northern and southern lights are sometimes called the polar auroras.

Dark and Clear Skies

Just being in the auroral oval does not guarantee a view of the northern lights. The skies must also be dark. There are always auroras in the skies. But just as stars are seen mainly at night, the northern lights are most visible after sunset when the sun's light is hidden.

In the far north, the sun does not set at all during the summer. Since it never gets dark, the northern lights are not visible in this "land of the midnight sun." The northern lights appear again in the fall, when days grow shorter and hours of darkness are longer.

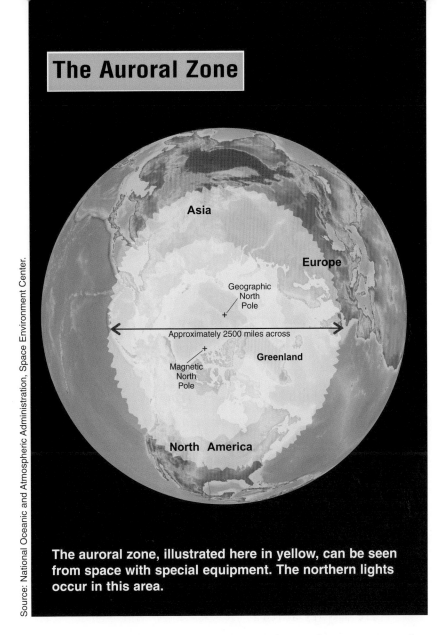

The Auroral Zone

Asia

Europe

Geographic
North
Pole

+

← Approximately 2500 miles across →

+

Magnetic
North
Pole

Greenland

North America

Source: National Oceanic and Atmospheric Administration, Space Environment Center.

The auroral zone, illustrated here in yellow, can be seen from space with special equipment. The northern lights occur in this area.

A cloudy sky also prevents viewers from seeing the northern lights. Sometimes the lights seem to circle the tops of mountains, or even brush the ground—but they do not. The lower edges of the northern lights are actually about sixty miles above the earth. Even though the northern lights might look close enough to touch, the bottom edges are really ten times higher than most airplanes fly.

Clouds form much lower than this, so the northern lights are not visible unless skies are clear.

A Noisy Show?

Many people say they have noticed whooshing, hissing, or crackling sounds during displays of the northern lights. These reports continue to puzzle researchers. So far no one has been able to record any sound from the northern lights. But even some of the scientists who study auroras have heard the noises.

In Lapland, which is a region of northern Europe, the name for the northern lights is *guovsahas*, which means

Northern lights may appear to touch the ground, but the lower edges of the lights are actually about sixty miles above Earth.

"light that can be heard." Native American and Inuit traditions also tell of noises that accompany the northern lights.

Some say the sound gets louder when the northern lights move and flicker. However, the lights are so high in the sky that any sounds they made would take about five minutes to travel down to Earth. If a curtain of lights made a crackling sound when it started to dance, people on the ground would not hear the sound when the curtain moved. They would hear the sound later, the same way the sound of a thunderclap follows the sight of a lightning bolt.

Maybe the strong magnetic and electrical fields that accompany the northern lights somehow make the noises on the ground, or even in the listeners' ears. Perhaps the noises are not related to the northern lights at all. Researchers continue to look for answers.

Capturing the Lights

The beauty of auroras has inspired artists and writers throughout history. Today's high-tech equipment helps people enjoy the northern lights in new ways. Special cameras take pictures of the northern lights from space, showing a glowing crown of light on top of the globe. Photographers check aurora forecasts on the Internet so they can figure out when to set up their cameras. Filmmakers capture auroras on film and video so that even people who live far from the north can enjoy the beauty of the northern lights.

Legends, Myths, and Mistakes

The northern lights lit up the night skies long before science could explain them. Over the centuries, people who lived in northern lands made up stories to explain the flickering colors in the heavens. In some of these stories, the northern lights were described as dancers or ball players. But in others, they were said to be evil spirits waiting to snatch young children or to tear peoples' eyes out.

Journey to the Lights

The Native Americans of the Pacific Northwest coast tell the story of Chief M'Sartto, Morning Star, who traveled to the northern lights. The chief's son would not play with the other boys in the tribe. Instead, he would slip away and disappear for days at a time. Curious about where his son went, the chief followed the boy. As he traveled, a strange feeling came over the chief. He felt like he was forgetting everything he knew. He closed his eyes and awoke in a country full of light.

In this new country, people were playing a ball game. They all wore lights on their heads and rainbow belts. As they played, the lights changed colors. The chief finally found his son playing ball with the others. After the game, Chief M'Sartto was introduced to the Chief of the Northern Lights. Then two large birds were

The early Native Americans of the Pacific Northwest made up stories to explain the northern lights. Some stories said the lights were a ball game in the sky.

called forth to carry the chief and his son home. During the journey, Chief M'Sartto forgot everything about the land of the northern lights, but his son remembered and continued to go there.

Ball Games and Dancing Spirits

Other cultures also believed that auroras were some sort of heavenly ball game. The native peoples of Greenland, Siberia, and parts of Canada thought the northern lights were the spirits of the dead playing ball with the head of a walrus. The residents of Nunivak Island, off the western coast of Alaska, gave this story a twist. They said the lights were walrus spirits playing ball with the head of a human!

To some, the colorful lights wheeling through the sky looked like dancing ghosts. In Scotland, the lights were called "merry dancers." Scots believed they were spirits fighting for the attention of a beautiful woman. In western Norway, people said the lights were old women dancing. As the women danced, they waved white mittens in the air. Other Scandinavians thought the lights were doing a lively dance called a polka.

The Inuit on the Yukon River said the dancers were not human spirits, but the spirits of deer, seals, fish, and whales. Other cultures also thought the lights were animals. The Danish believed that swans had flown too far north and gotten frozen in the ice. The lights were supposedly the reflections from the swans' flapping wings. The Chippewa in Canada believed that a bright aurora meant that many deer were in the sky. This belief may have come from the fact that if someone strokes a deer in the dark, static electricity can make sparks fly.

Some cultures believed the northern lights were dancing ghosts.

Fires, Battles, and Warnings

Many Native American cultures believed the flickering northern lights were fires in the heavens. The Makah of Washington State thought a race of dwarves lived in the sky. The dwarves were only half as tall as a canoe paddle, but they were so strong that they could catch whales with their bare hands. They boiled the blubber from the whales over the fires in the sky. The Menominee of Wisconsin thought the lights were from the torches of friendly giants. The giants used the torches to help them spear fish at night. To the Mandan of North Dakota, the northern lights were fires burning under the big pots in which medicine men and warriors cooked their enemies.

When northern lights appeared red, many Native Americans believed they were fires in the heavens.

The northern lights can look so much like fire that they have caused many false alarms throughout history. In A.D. 37, the emperor of Rome believed an aurora was actually a burning town. He sent soldiers to rescue townspeople, but the rescuers found no fire. When red flames appeared in the skies over London in 1839, people feared that Windsor Castle was burning. Practically every fire engine in London was sent to respond. The fire turned out to be a red aurora glowing in the night sky.

People also associated red auroras with blood and battles. Finlanders thought the lights were a fierce fight between the archangel Michael and the devil. Other Scandinavians thought the lights were reflections from the shields of the Valkyries, a legendary race of fierce female warriors. According to myths, these warriors descended from the sky and decided which mortals would die in battles. Many believed that the northern lights predicted war. Some Native Americans feared the lights were the ghosts of defeated enemies trying to come back for revenge.

Since the northern lights are not usually visible in much of Europe, their appearance sometimes caused widespread panic. In 1583 when people in France saw fires in the sky, they were convinced that God was angry with them. Thousands traveled to churches in Paris to make offerings and pray.

Northern Lights Superstitions

Many cultures had superstitions about the northern lights. The Vidda of northern Norway believed that if a child made fun of the northern lights, the lights would come down from the sky and kill the child. Inuit made their children come inside when the lights shone. They were afraid the spirits wanted to steal their children's heads and use them for balls in their heavenly ball game.

In northern Europe, the Lapps believed it was dangerous to whistle at the lights. They also warned against looking at the lights for too long, fearing that the lights could come down and tear out their eyes. During northern lights displays, women covered their heads when they went outside because they believed that the lights could swoop down and grab their hair.

The Lapps were also careful not to use sleigh bells or make loud noises in their homes when the northern lights shone brightly. Elling Carlsen, who worked as an ice pilot on boats in the 1800s, made sure he was not wearing or carrying any metal when he sailed in northern seas. He believed the metal might provoke the northern lights.

In Iceland, people thought that if a pregnant woman looked at the lights, her child would be born with crossed eyes. In northern Norway, people were warned not to wave at the lights; to do so would attract the lights to Earth, where they would come down and cause trouble.

But in some places, people tried to attract the northern lights. Some Scandinavians waved white sheets at them in hopes of getting them to sparkle more. Others thought that whistling at the lights would bring them down to Earth or make them shine more brightly.

Scientific Theories

While some cultures explained the lights as ball games and dancers, scientists tried to find logical explanations

Many cultures had superstitions about the northern lights and tried to avoid them.

for them. Many thought the northern lights were caused by sunlight reflecting off the ice crystals in the north. Galileo Galilei, the seventeenth-century astronomer, believed they were vapor rising from the earth and lit up by the sun. He called the lights *boreale aurora*, which means "northern dawn." This is where the name *aurora borealis* comes from.

Benjamin Franklin correctly believed the northern lights were electrical in nature. Some observed that auroras were linked to spots on the sun. Others noticed that during auroras, compass needles jumped. These are pieces of the puzzle, but it was not until quite recently that scientists understood how all the pieces fit together.

CHAPTER THREE

What Causes the Northern Lights?

What causes these natural fireworks? In the last fifty years, much has been learned about the northern lights. With the telescopes, instruments, and spacecraft that are available now, scientists can test their ideas and see which are correct. They now know that for the northern lights to shine, three things are needed: moving charged particles, a magnetic field, and an **atmosphere**.

Wind from the Sun

Although the northern lights flicker in the skies overhead, their story actually begins 93 million miles away on the sun.

The sun, like other stars, is a ball of burning gases. The surface of the sun is extremely hot, but the fiery **corona** that surrounds the sun is even hotter—nearly

2 million degrees Fahrenheit! The sun is made up mostly of helium and hydrogen atoms. The corona is so hot that the atoms cannot hold together. The atoms break down into particles, which boil off and fly out in all directions. Scientists call these particles from the sun the **solar wind**.

Solar wind particles fly off the surface of the sun. When the particles reach the earth's atmosphere, northern lights form.

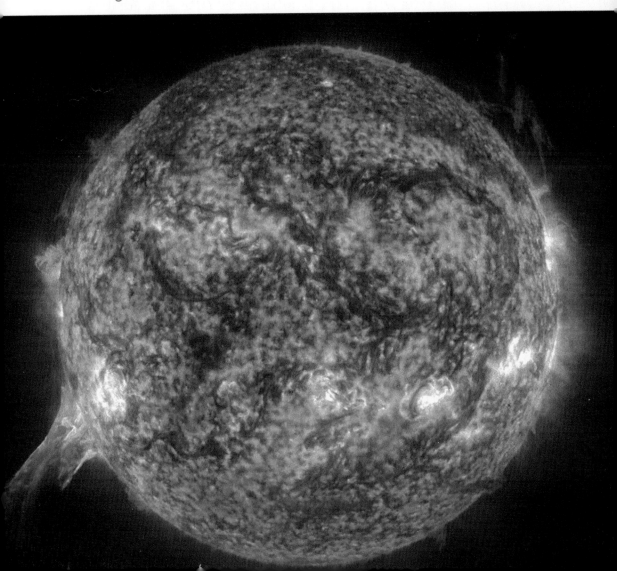

A car on a freeway travels about sixty miles per hour. Solar wind particles speed away from the sun at around nine hundred thousand miles per hour! The sun has a magnetic field, and the particles carry the sun's magnetic field with them out into the solar system. After several days, some of the solar wind particles approach another magnetic field: the one that surrounds the earth.

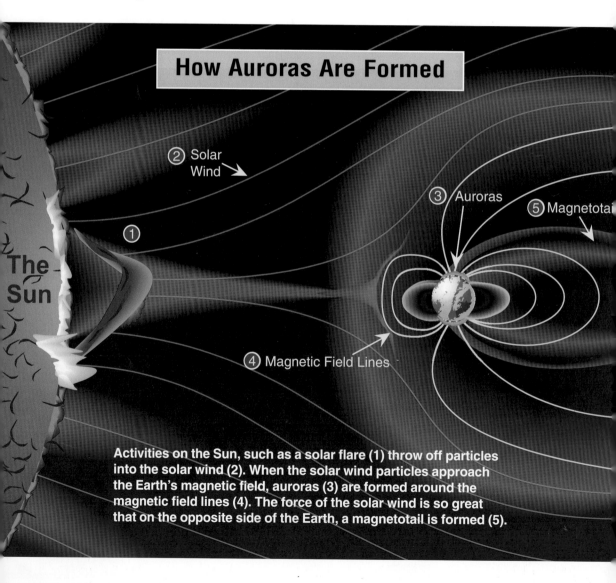

How Auroras Are Formed

② Solar Wind

③ Auroras

⑤ Magnetotail

①

The Sun

④ Magnetic Field Lines

Activities on the Sun, such as a solar flare (1) throw off particles into the solar wind (2). When the solar wind particles approach the Earth's magnetic field, auroras (3) are formed around the magnetic field lines (4). The force of the solar wind is so great that on the opposite side of the Earth, a magnetotail is formed (5).

A Giant Magnet

The center of the earth is partly made up of melted iron. The movement of this liquid metal creates an invisible magnetic field that surrounds the earth like a bubble. The earth acts as if a huge bar magnet is inside it. The north and south **geomagnetic poles** are where the ends of the bar magnet would be. They are not the same as the north and south geographic poles. The north geomagnetic pole is in Greenland, and is the center of the auroral oval. The earth's magnetic field loops from one geomagnetic pole to the other.

The solar wind is so strong that it squashes the earth's magnetic field on the side of the earth facing the sun. On the side of the earth away from the sun, the solar wind pulls the earth's magnetic field out into a long tail. This tail, called the **magnetotail**, stretches over 850,000 miles away from the earth—more than three times the distance from the earth to the moon.

The earth's magnetic field protects the planet, shielding it from most of the solar wind. But when the earth's magnetic field and the sun's magnetic field that is carried by the solar particles line up in the right way, the fields join together. Then solar wind particles can cross into the earth's magnetic field. The earth's magnetic field pushes some of the particles in one direction and some in another. The separation of these particles causes electric currents to flow through the earth's magnetic field.

Most of the particles that cause the aurora enter the field through the magnetotail. They join other particles that are trapped in the magnetic field. Some of the trapped particles speed up and shoot toward the earth. The particles follow the lines of the earth's magnetic field and mostly end up in the auroral ovals. But the particles alone do not cause the northern lights.

Sea of Gases

An ocean of gases surrounds the earth. These gases are called the atmosphere. When solar wind particles enter the atmosphere, they collide with the atoms and molecules that make up the atmosphere. After a particle hits an atom, the atom gives off light.

The northern lights work in the same way that a neon light does. A neon light is made by filling a glass tube with a gas. When a stream of charged particles is shot through the tube, the particles hit the gas atoms and the atoms give off light. The color of light depends on the type of gas in the tube. Neon gas gives off red light, and sodium gives off yellow light. Other gases produce other colors.

The northern lights shine with different colors, depending upon which gases in the atmosphere are being hit by the solar wind particles. Most of the atmosphere is made up of oxygen and nitrogen atoms and molecules. Oxygen atoms give off either a red or green light, depending upon how hard they are hit. Nitrogen molecules give off either red or blue light.

Stormy Space Weather

Because solar particles cause the northern lights, the more particles the sun gives off, the brighter the

displays are likely to be. The sun is always boiling off particles into the solar wind. But when the sun is stormy, even more particles shoot off into space.

The different colors of northern lights are caused by solar wind particles hitting different types of gases in the earth's atmosphere.

Sometimes huge explosions on the sun's surface fling out particles. These explosions are called **solar flares.** If a solar flare is on the side of the sun facing the earth, its particles can make the northern lights shine more brightly. **Coronal mass ejections** are explosions in the sun's outer atmosphere. These super-sized eruptions hurl billions of tons of solar material into space at speeds of about 1 million miles per hour.

Both solar flares and coronal mass ejections are linked to sunspots. Sunspots are dark areas on the surface of the sun. When there are more sunspots, there are more solar flares and more coronal mass ejections. By keeping track of the sunspot cycle, scientists can predict when the northern lights will be most active.

Changes in the sun's magnetic field can cause changes in the northern lights. In large areas called **coronal holes**, the sun's magnetic field is weaker than in the surrounding areas. Solar particles escape through the weakened field and shoot into space. These coronal holes can last for months. The sun spins on its axis about once every twenty-seven days. If a coronal hole causes the northern lights to shine brightly, there is a good chance that the lights will be bright again twenty-seven days later when the same part of the sun faces the earth.

Auroras on Other Planets

Earth is not the only planet with auroras. Jupiter, Saturn, Uranus, and Neptune have magnetic fields and atmospheres, so they have auroras as well.

Solar flares erupt from the sun's surface. When facing Earth, solar flares make the northern lights shine more brightly.

Advances in technology helped scientists learn about the northern lights. But as humans became dependent on technology, the northern lights began to create unexpected problems.

CHAPTER FOUR

Danger Signs

The northern lights provide viewers with a spectacular show. However, the beautiful lights dancing through the skies can signal problems down on Earth. During northern lights displays, power and communication systems can fail. The northern lights can produce electrical currents that corrode oil and natural-gas pipelines. The earth's magnetic field changes when the northern lights shine, so compasses may be unreliable. Even the satellites circling in the skies above the earth can be affected by the northern lights and the solar storms that cause them.

Cut-Off Communication

When the northern lights are active, very strong electrical currents travel through the sky because the particles carry an electrical charge. These electrical currents cause

When northern lights are active, strong electrical currents are created on Earth. The currents can flow through power and telephone lines disrupting service.

changes in the earth's magnetic field. The changes in the magnetic field can **induce**, or create, electrical currents on Earth. These currents can flow through telephone lines, power lines, and long pipelines.

The problems caused by the northern lights were obvious even back in the 1800s. In the days before telephones were invented, people relied on telegraph machines to send messages over long distances. The messages were sent through telegraph wires that stretched from city to city.

Telegraph operators found that during brilliant auroras, strange electrical currents flowed through their telegraph wires. These currents made communication unreliable. The currents could scramble messages people were trying to send. Sparks sometimes flew out of the telegraph equipment. In some cases, communication was cut off completely. Sometimes the current was so strong that the telegraph operators were able to send messages without using their batteries!

In later years, the northern lights wreaked havoc with telephone communication as well. Currents generated in the telephone wires could be so strong that they blew out fuses in telephone circuits and shut down communications.

The northern lights can also disrupt radio broadcasts. After radio waves are sent out, they travel up until they reach the **ionosphere,** which is the outer part of the earth's atmosphere. Usually, the ionosphere bounces the radio waves back to Earth, where they are then picked up by receivers. But during northern lights displays, the ionosphere changes. It no longer reliably reflects the waves back to Earth. This means that during auroras, radio signals can be weak or garbled. Sometimes they even disappear completely.

Blackout!

In 1989 the sunspot cycle was at its peak and auroras were bright. On March 13 of that year, the northern lights shone in stunning beauty over Alaska and northern Europe. Most people in Quebec, a province in Canada, were in bed at 2:45 A.M. that night. But anyone looking out the window at that hour would have seen the streetlights suddenly blink out. Refrigerators stopped running, and radios and televisions were silenced.

Almost 6 million people lost their electricity that evening. By 6 A.M., the power company in Quebec had bought enough electricity from the United States to turn some of the lights back on. However, many people in Quebec were without power until after noon that day—over nine hours.

What caused the blackout? The northern lights caused currents to run through the long power lines that stretch across the country. When these lines get overloaded, safety switches open and the power is shut off. This is what happened in Quebec. Similar power outages have occurred in other northern areas.

Pipeline Damage

Not only communications and power are affected by auroras. Just a few months after the blackout in Canada, a gas pipeline exploded near the Trans-Siberian Railroad. Two passenger trains on the railroad at the time were set on fire. More than one thousand people were rescued from the flames, but five hundred people died.

The strong electrical currents created by northern lights have been known to disrupt radio transmissions, telephone service, and electricity.

Scientists believe that currents associated with the northern lights flowed through the pipeline. Over time, these currents caused the pipeline to corrode and leak more quickly than it should have. People now take solar activity and the northern lights into account when they design pipelines that will be used in the north. The Alaska oil pipeline was specially designed to reduce the damage that auroras can cause.

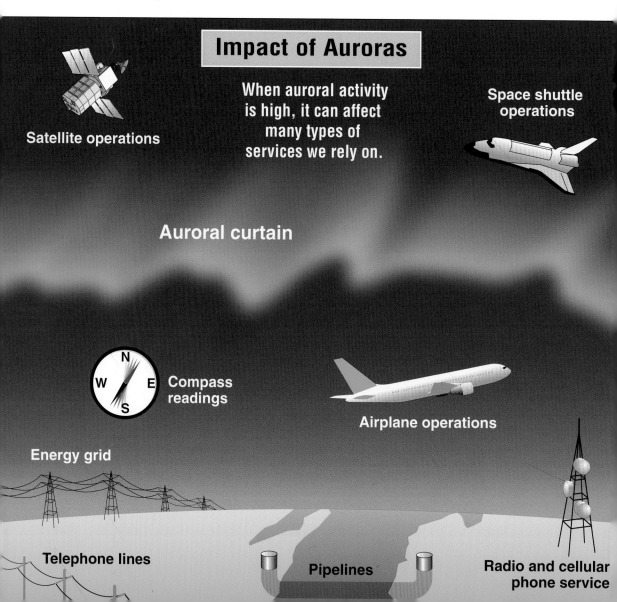

Impact of Auroras

When auroral activity is high, it can affect many types of services we rely on.

Satellite operations

Space shuttle operations

Auroral curtain

Compass readings

Airplane operations

Energy grid

Telephone lines

Pipelines

Radio and cellular phone service

Electrical currents from northern lights have caused damage to pipelines. Now pipes are specially designed for use in northern regions where the lights shine.

Other Problems

Even compasses on the ground and satellites in the skies can be affected by the northern lights. Compasses point to the north because of the earth's magnetic field. When northern lights are very active, the earth's magnetic field is disturbed, and compasses may point the wrong way. Although they may be wrong by only a degree or two, this can be enough to cause problems.

The activity of northern lights can disturb the earth's magnetic field, causing problems with compasses.

In the past, these compass errors may have caused shipwrecks. Today surveyors use magnetic readings when they search for minerals, oil, and gases in the earth. If magnetic disturbances are not taken into account, the maps they make might not be correct. This could lead to expensive mistakes, such as drilling for oil in the wrong place.

Intense northern lights displays can heat the upper atmosphere. The heat makes the upper atmosphere expand. This can increase the atmosphere's drag on satellites orbiting the earth, shortening their lives. The particles from the strong solar wind that causes bright auroras can get into satellites and damage the delicate equipment inside them.

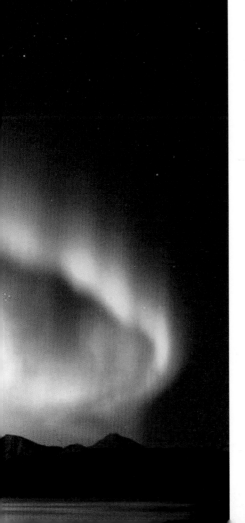

Searching for Solutions

Because of the problems that are associated with solar storms and the northern lights, scientists are working to learn how to predict them. If people know when a storm is on the way, they can take steps to protect equipment and communication systems.

Satellites in the skies now help give warning of approaching storms. Solar researchers keep track of activity on the surface of the sun. Aurora scientists launch rockets into the atmosphere to gather information about the northern lights and the earth's magnetic field.

Despite years of research, many questions about the northern lights remain unanswered. Until science better understands them, the northern lights will continue to combine great beauty with a hint of danger.

Glossary

atmosphere: The sea of gases that surrounds a planet or a star.

auroral oval: The area where auroras are occurring at any given time.

auroral zone: The parts of the world where auroras are most likely to happen.

corona: The sun's outer atmosphere.

coronal holes: Parts of the sun with weak magnetic fields that allow more particles to escape.

coronal mass ejections: Explosions in the sun's corona that push huge amounts of solar material into space.

geomagnetic poles: The places where the ends of the imaginary bar magnet in the earth would be.

induce: Cause to occur.

ionosphere: The earth's outer atmosphere.

magnetotail: The part of the earth's magnetic field that the solar wind pulls out into space.

solar flares: Explosions on the surface of the sun.

solar wind: Particles from the sun that boil off and fly out into space.

For Further Exploration

Books

Roy A. Gallant, *Rainbows, Mirages and Sundogs: The Sky as a Source of Wonder.* New York: Macmillan, 1987. Clear explanations of the northern lights, eclipses, and other phenomena in the sky.

Calvin Hall and Daryl Pederson (essay by George Bryson), *Northern Lights: The Science, Myth, and Wonder of Aurora Borealis.* Seattle: Sasquatch Books, 2001. Spectacular pictures of northern lights displays.

Web Sites

Exploratorium (www.exploratorium.edu). This Web site includes a section entitled "Auroras: Paintings in the Sky" which offers lots of information about auroras including some good photographs.

Nordlys: Northern Lights (www.northern-lights.no). Lots of information and photos from a Norwegian research facility. Follow the "What causes them?" link on the left to see an animation of solar particles caught in the earth's magnetic field.

SpaceWeather.com (www.spaceweather.com). This site gives aurora forecasts and current solar wind conditions, as well as information about solar flares and coronal holes.

Index

Picture Credits

Cover image: © Cary Anderson/CORBIS Sygma
© AFP/CORBIS, 29
Cary Anderson/Aurora, 32
© Bjorn Backe; Papilio/CORBIS, 37
© Raymond Gehman/CORBIS, 15
© Images.com/CORBIS, 14
Patrick Pleul/EPA/Landov, 17, 18
Reuters/Landov, 23
Hinrich B. Semann/DPA/Landov, 7, 38–39
© Tim Thompson/CORBIS, 21
David Tipling/Lonely Planet Images, 8, 35
© Kennan Ward/CORBIS, 26–27

About the Author

Deborah Underwood writes nonfiction, fiction, and poetry for children. She grew up in Walla Walla, Washington, and received a bachelor's degree in philosophy from Pomona College in Claremont, California. She now lives in San Francisco. When she is not writing, she enjoys reading and singing in a chamber choir.